Self-Leadership
for Success

Achieving Success through a
Strategic Journey of Self-Mastery

Marichen M Mortimer

Self-Leadership for Success

Achieving Success through a Strategic Journey of Self-Mastery

I believe in learning by doing, reflecting, sharing and continuously sculpting ourselves and our lives, thereby being open to the creative process of living. We are ultimately not in charge of our lives; however we are in charge of what we choose and even in the choosing we dance a creative dance of exploration, better enjoyed if we can maintain a sense of wonderment at what unfolds. Life is after all about the journey and not the destination. So enjoy your travels.

Marichen M Mortimer

This book is dedicated to my beloved son Yurie Alexander, with whom I have journeyed from "Antarctica to Bora Bora". You are my true soul travelling partner and make my life shine.

To my mom and late dad, for your loving support and encouragement.

Knowing yourself is an imperative for success.

Contents

Foreword

I had the pleasure of attending Marichen's "Self-Leadership for Success" course as an observer. Originally I planned to introduce her, observe for a while and then leave for my other pressing engagements. After listening to her for a couple of minutes I was hooked. Needless to say I sent my Professional Assistant a message asking if it was possible to reschedule my diary for the day. She managed to free up a couple of hours. I found myself totally immersed in Marichen, her subject material and the way she made sense of self leadership for and with the participants. I guess I took the time to be quiet and still, reflecting with the participants, ignoring my crazy schedule for a couple of hours.

I hope you will enjoy the book as much as I enjoyed the "movie"! I certainly enjoyed both and as with any good book or movie, I can't wait for the sequel to be released!

Marichen, I wish you success and happiness; please continue the fantastic work you are doing.

All the best

Reinette Van der Merwe

Managing Director

Barclays Bank of Botswana

Acknowledgements

To my many clients without whom this book would never have seen the light of day, thank you for pushing me to write. I hope you enjoy the end result.

To my dearest friends, thank you for being there and supporting and encouraging me always.

To my clients and friends who are also my continuous teachers, I humbly learn from you.

To Marius de Jongh, thank you for your critical proofreading and your continuous support.

To Brian Kearney-Grieve, thank you my dear friend for your creative input and proofreading.

To Peter Southey, thank you for your thorough proofreading and advice.

To Tracey Dobrin, you are the best creative friend I could ask for; thank you for the beautiful cover design.

To Rich Simmonds, thank you for your encouragement, advice and guidance.

To Marina Snyman, thank you for the final editing, layout and end product.

dearest

Chapter 1. Introduction

This book is not intended as an academic work, nor do I wish to compete with the myriad of self-help books available. Rather its purpose is to go on a journey with the reader, a journey of self-discovery, to gain insights and to provoke thinking around how we can be all that we are placed on Earth to be.

The content message is based on my years of working in the corporate environment in various industries, ranging from manufacturing to the IT industry, and working across functions from marketing to strategy, including leadership development. It is in the arena of leadership development, management and executive coaching that I noticed that it is really necessary for leaders to get to know themselves very intimately before they are able to lead authentically and from an inner place of guidance, as opposed to an outer place of force, as this is not sustainable in the long run. It is on this experience, and over years of observations of what makes truly resilient leaders and effective managers, that I have developed this book.

I therefore dedicate the book to all those who have crossed my path, with whom I have had conversations, and who sincerely seek to be the best they can be and to make a conscious choice to make a positive contribution to the world. We are all teachers and learners to each other.

dearest

Chapter 2. The invitation to the journey

"The first move toward mastery is always inward – learning who you really are and reconnecting with that innate force."

- Robert Greene

Dearest reader, welcome to this journey. This is your journey - a journey to get to know yourself better so that you can be the best that you can be in all the spheres of your life that you choose. I wish in the process that you become a beloved soul of the universe. If you are going to make the necessary shifts to be the best that you can be, to yourself and others, you can only do so when you recognise yourself as a beloved soul. When we feel good about ourselves, we are able to offer that gift to ourselves and to others as well. I also believe that to be whole people we need to address all aspects of ourselves to create some form of equilibrium. If you are skilled at maths but can't dance, then attempt another form of creative pursuit such as cooking, gardening, painting, writing or woodwork. The list is endless and the outcome of feeling and being whole is deeply satisfying. (By whole I mean properly connecting into all our human aspects - mental, physical, emotional, spiritual and creative.)

This journey is a wonderful unique journey, because you have probably never walked it before. So I invite you to take some quiet time on your own while you immerse yourself in the book, so that you can be uninterrupted, allowing yourself some graceful space to question and reflect where you need to in order to **discover** aspects of yourself that may have been hidden until now.

I invite you to have:

- An open mind to allow for exploration
- A good sense of humour to allow for a non-judgemental state of mind
- A sense of wonder to allow for self-discovery
- A sense of **innocence** so as to keep the ego excluded from your journey process
- Time to allow yourself to explore and reflect
- Commitment to honour yourself by being totally honest with yourself
- Patience to allow yourself to learn

And so we start our journey... The book is structured in such a way that it gives you context for the journey; we then explore self-leadership and the various aspects of it and we end with some thoughts for your next steps. Each chapter has an introduction, the shared journey and then some self-reflection questions. It is suggested that you read this book with a journal and make your notes on your self-reflection questions as you progress. This way you will gain the maximum personal benefit. The more you put into the process, the more you will get **out**. Guaranteed.

Enjoy the journey.

Naviche.

Chapter 3. Setting the context of choice

"Everyone holds his fortune in his own hands, like a sculptor the
raw material he will fashion into a figure. But it's the same with
that type of artistic activity as with all others: We are merely born
with the capability to do it. The skill to mould the material into what
we want must be learned and attentively cultivated."

- Johann Wolfgang von Goethe

When we set out on a journey, we would like to know where
we are going. This journey with me is no different to that. This
journey, however, is one that will take you inwards. Given that
we work in organisations where we are constantly chasing
deadlines, performance targets and the like, we are not used to
being quiet and still. This feels counterintuitive because we
have stopped practising this vital skill which existed in our
forebears and which we are losing day by day as we run on the
treadmill we call our lives.

So, you are asked you to be patient and take time to be still. It
is only in stillness that we can tap into our intuitive voice, our
true guiding light.

A few questions to consider:

- Have you ever battled to make a critical decision while
  experiencing a battle between your heart and mind, and
  you then chose the option provided by the mind and it
  backfired?

15

- Have you ever felt disconnected from your feelings and if people ask you how you feel, your answer starts with: "I think…."?
- Have you ever experienced your mind taking you into a downward spiral of despair and you continue following this negative flow of thoughts?

So in order to create a full context, the following will be shared with you in this chapter:

- How to create a positive inner context daily
- The power of commitment
- What happens to us when we are faced with change, and the impact of the choices we make - reactive and creative
- Our intent
- The art and science of relaxation

Imagine the following scenario. You are in a team; I give each one of you a bag of mango pips with the instruction to go to Antarctica and plant them and to contact me as soon as they are growing. The plane leaves and off you go. Weeks go by and I don't hear from you. Then I call you and you inform me that there was no luck as the soil conditions are too tough and it is impossible to get the mango pips to grow unless you go the hothouse route. I respond that this is no problem: I am sending the company jet to collect everyone and we have a further surprise: you are now all going to Bora Bora.

I give each of you fresh mango pips and ask you to plant them and to contact me with the results. You are all ecstatic, but upon arriving in the paradise-like conditions of Bora Bora you toss the bag of mango pips aside and head for the bar where you order yourself a cool drink and thoroughly enjoy the place. When I call you a few weeks later you guiltily pretend that there is a bad signal and you put the phone down. Then you hastily retrace your steps to where you discarded the pips and to your amazement you find that the mango pips have grown into the beginnings of small trees! You call me immediately and I order the plane to bring you all back: mission accomplished! I ask you all upon your return: "So what happened?"   The conclusion is that the conditions were conducive for the mango pips to grow in Bora Bora and not in Antarctica.

Life is very similar; when we don't create the environment that is conducive to allow growth, no growth will take place. Similarly, when we embark on our inner journey we need to create the inner conditions to allow for personal growth to take place. In order to do so we need to make a choice. Will we be creating **Antarctic** conditions for ourselves or Bora Bora conditions? ......but know this: When we choose we commit.

So how do we create Bora Bora conditions?

When we wake up in the morning the first thing we become aware of is our thoughts and we can choose our context for the day. To create Bora Bora conditions for ourselves we can decide, for example: "I will be positive throughout my day, no matter what. I know that I have the wherewithal to deal with each and every challenge in a positive way." Or you can decide something simple: "I choose to be positive". Then during the day, whether things are tough or not, remind yourself of your early morning commitment and check in with yourself to see how you are doing. Keep yourself on track. Remind yourself of your commitment to remain positive.

Some true words by W.H. Murray about commitment: "*Until one is committed...there is hesitancy, the chance to draw back, always ineffectiveness. Concerning all acts of initiative (and creation) there is one elemental truth, the ignorance of which kills countless ideas and splendid plans: that the moment one definitely commits oneself, the Providence moves, too. All sorts of things occur to help one that would never otherwise have occurred. A whole stream of events issues from the decision, raising in one's favour all manner of unforeseen incidents and material assistance, which no man could have dreamt would have come his way.*"

When you commit fully, in the words of the late Stephen Covey: "*The more involved you are, the more significant your learning will be.*"

Our next concept to understand in this journey is what happens to us when we are faced with change?

- Do we resist it **outright,** because it makes us feel uncomfortable?
- Do we embrace it and say: "Bring it on"?
- Do we pretend it is not happening and bury our heads deep in the sand and wait for it to go away?

Your personal response to change could be any one of these or a combination of two of them or something quite different.

It will vary according to your past experiences, for example, or to your current state of mind or the perceived risks associated with the required change. What is crucial is that you are aware of your own particular response to change and aware, too, that you have the ability to choose your response in a given situation.

The following diagram of the U-curve of change is based on the work of Otto Scharmer. He argues that the stages in the response to change are predictable for humans in general, although at any time different people will find themselves at different stages of this cycle. The most important requirement is to acknowledge that they are inevitable and natural. Going through them is the way humans adapt and adjust.

The U-Curve of Change

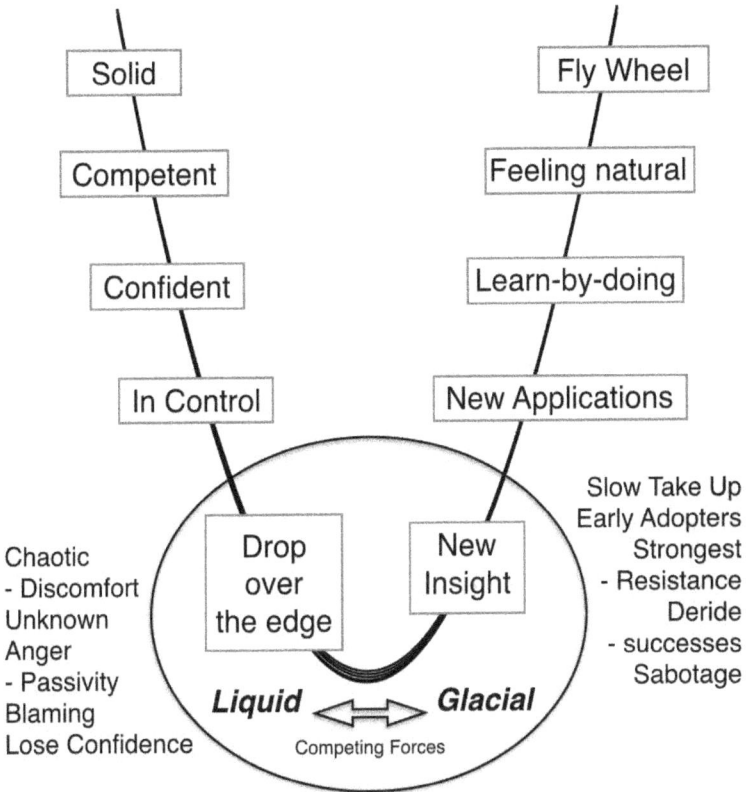

Solid

Competent

Confident

In Control

Fly Wheel

Feeling natural

Learn-by-doing

New Applications

Drop over the edge

New Insight

Chaotic
- Discomfort
Unknown
Anger
- Passivity
Blaming
Lose Confidence

Slow Take Up
Early Adopters
Strongest
- Resistance
Deride
- successes
Sabotage

Liquid ⟷ *Glacial*
Competing Forces

The left side of the curve shows us when we feel competent and in charge before we are confronted with the change. As we are faced with the impact of the change we slide down the curve, dropping over the edge, as it were, and we go into the liquid phase, where we experience a variety of emotions, ranging from uncertainty to anger. As we adjust we slowly start moving up the curve as we gain confidence. We can sometimes experience another slide downward, only to move upwards again, until we have mastered whatever the change was about.

For example, in business we could be facing a buy-out which would bring about a change in corporate culture, a change in who the boss would be and in possible working conditions. At this point we are faced with choices: we can leave and seek other employment or we can stay and choose how we will face the challenges. When we choose to stay, we move into the U-curve of change and make choices all along the way which influence our behaviour.

On a personal level, change could be anything from moving house, to starting or ending a relationship, or starting a family or losing a loved one.

When we are faced with change we are also faced with the **possibility** of personal transformation. So briefly, for the purpose of our journey, the simple definitions of transformation and change are:

Transformation means to alter in **character** or **condition** to another differing form.

With 'Change' I simply refer to the substitution of one thing for another.

Transformation occurs when we reflect on our behavior and feelings and reflect on the responses we receive when we interact with other people both on a personal and a professional level. Transforming the way we think, feel and act will enable us to expand our inherent potential. Effective transformation requires balancing mind, body and soul. Imbalance leads to a loss of meaning, stifled creativity, a loss of productivity and stress that most often results in illness.

When we transform positively we allow for personal growth to take place. As when a caterpillar transforms into a butterfly, it is never an easy or a comfortable process, but the beauty that results is well worth the effort.

Self–leadership requires one to endure plateaus while learning to enjoy the journey and to find joy in the gain this brings. Transformation requires long-term, self-regulating, disciplined activities fed by regular honest feedback from others. When we are faced with choices we have the opportunity to choose to be either reactive or creative. As Victor Frankl so powerfully said: *"Between stimulus and response lies the freedom to choose"*

When we react automatically or emotionally we engage the amygdala of the brain. We then go into fight, flight or freeze mode, and respond with anger, denial, blame and withdrawal. When we respond creatively we engage the neocortex, responding in a co-creative, heartfelt and rational manner. It is important to keep these acts in mind when we are confronted with change, and to watch our bodies and emotions and what these reveal to us about how we feel.

This brings us to ask ourselves the question: "When I respond, what is my intent?" In other words, what is the place where I am coming from? Is it a place of: "I am okay and you are okay; we can explore possibilities together to solve the challenges"? Is it a place of: "I am okay and you are not; I will therefore tell you what we will do", or is it "You know best, you are more competent and I feel threatened but I will still force my decision and we will go in my direction"? When we walk the path of self-leadership, we become aware of the intent of our choices and the resultant behaviours, and the impact our intent has on the choices we make. We ultimately need to take accountability and responsibility for the choices we make and even the ones we choose not to make.

"Successful leadership depends on the quality of attention and intention that the leader brings to any situation. Two leaders in the same circumstances doing the same thing can bring about completely different outcomes, depending on the inner place from which each operates." - Otto Scharmer (Otto Scharmer is a senior lecturer at Massachusetts Institute of Technology's Sloan School of Management)

Finally, our last context creation topic is **relaxation.** You may ask yourself, why on earth relaxation?

Let me share a personal experience, and I am sure you will be able to share many related ones as well. In my first year at university, on day one of our accounting lectures, I walked in and the lecturer said in a very threatening tone: "Look to your left and look to your right. Only one of you three will pass these exams at the end of the year". This was not exactly an invitation to relax and learn the course to the best of your ability. Needless to say, the lecturer had me nervous from the initial **moment** and things never got better thereafter. He was unapproachable when I needed assistance to progress and in general I felt myself shut down towards the subject. I did not pass it at the end of the year. I deregistered from it and changed course.

Many years later, as I was doing my Masters degree, I had to do accounting again. On day one of the course I went to the lecturer afterwards and told him that I had to pass this course. I said I was prepared to work very hard but if I encountered difficulty I needed to know whether he would be available to **assist**. He looked at me in utter surprise and responded with: "Of course, that is my job." I shared with him my undergraduate experience and am pleased to say that he made the course so interesting that I passed the year with distinction.

This example illustrates a number of things - the intent of the two lecturers differed vastly and they thereby created two very different learning environments. The one created a tense, "only one out of three will make it" environment, whereas the other created an environment of "I will do my duty and make it interesting, and of course you can pass." They both got their respective results, as did I. I learned an important lesson, namely that when we create a positive, relaxed, learning environment and allow ourselves and others to grow, we are more likely to achieve positive results. However, when we are tense it takes us longer to learn and our **retention** of information is not as good as when we are relaxed.

Moreover, it is now a researched medical fact that stress lies beneath many modern day medical conditions and the severity thereof.

Thus, **relaxation** is imperative, but how can we relax? Relaxation is both an art and a science. It occurs when we are able to let go of all expectations and connect with our senses in order to focus the mind and to become quiet. Science has taught us methods that we can apply to learn to relax.

The following is a relaxation exercise which you need to take your time with and do slowly:

Find a quiet place where you won't be disturbed.

Sit quietly in your chair with your back up straight. Place your feet comfortably on the ground. Place your hands on your thighs. Close your eyes. Become aware of your whole body where you are sitting. Become aware of your breathing. Feel the expansion in your chest as you breathe in and the contraction in your chest as you breathe out. Start to breathe slowly, in and out. Allow your breathing to become deeper and more relaxed. Now progress your awareness to your body. Consciously and with focus relax your shoulders, your arms and then your abdomen. Take a slow deep breath and relax your stomach area completely. Relax your legs. Now, mentally scan your whole body and on the next inhalation and exhalation, relax your entire being. Visualise yourself feeling totally relaxed and sitting in a beautiful garden, surrounded by roses. Visualise one particular beautiful pink rose. See this rose as clearly as you possibly can. If you can, even smell its sweet, fresh fragrance. Enjoy the feeling and relax completely. Be in the moment admiring the rose, while feeling deeply relaxed. Now, take your awareness to your feet. Wiggle your toes and place them back on the ground. When you feel ready to return to the here and now, slowly become aware of your body sitting in the chair. Take a deep breath in and out and open your eyes.

Summary box:

In conclusion, one can see how important it is to create the necessary environment both internally and externally to ensure that you achieve the results you are interested in for your own growth. To create the inner context – daily choose between barren Antarctica and fertile Bora Bora. State your positive statement, for example, "I commit to being positive" and write it down and put it somewhere so that you are reminded of that during the day. Fully commit to your choice and see how the universe conspires to make things happen accordingly and if you are faced with challenges, how you handle them differently.

Be aware of your choices and whether you are being reactive or creative in making them.

Our intent from which we operate is critical as it directly determines how we conduct ourselves; choose your intent with awareness.

Consciously relax and create an environment that is relaxed if you want yourself and others to learn.

dearest

Chapter 4. Self-leadership

"The intuitive mind is a sacred gift and the rational mind is a faithful servant. We have created a society that honours the servant and has forgotten the gift."

- Albert Einstein

In this chapter, our journey will take us to a few of the key qualities required to deepen our self-leadership skills, and then we will encounter the self-leadership wheel, which looks at overall wellness. There are self-reflection questions at the end of each section. Do not rush through them; take your time and enjoy getting to know yourself better through a gentle lens of understanding.

The following is a story of a mother who takes her diabetic child to see her guru, Gandhi. The mother and son spend hours standing in the queue. When they finally reach the front of the queue the mother explains to Ghandi that her son is ill with diabetes and asks him for his advice. Gandhi asks them to very kindly return next week. She is nonplussed, but returns home with her son. The following week they repeat the process and when they finally reach the front of the queue she repeats her request, whereupon Gandhi replies: "Tell him to stop eating sugar." She says "Guru, why did you not tell me this last week?" He replied: "Because last week I was still eating sugar."

The moral of the story is clear. We cannot expect others to do what we are not willing to do ourselves. How often in the workplace do we demand that others do what we are not willing to do ourselves? What are the results we have experienced?

We need to understand that leadership is all about walking the talk and leading by example and we cannot exclude this principle from self-leadership.

Self-leadership is having a developed sense of who you are, what you can do, and where you are going, coupled with the ability to influence your communication, emotions and behaviour on the way to getting there. In the words of Lao Tzu: "Mastering others is strength. Mastering yourself is true power." (Lao Tzu is regarded as the father of the Tao Te Ching. According to legend he was the keeper of the archives at the imperial court. When he was eighty years old he set out for the western border of China, toward what is now Tibet, saddened and disillusioned that men were unwilling to follow the path to natural goodness. At the border (Hank Pass), a guard, Yin Xi (Yin Hsi), asked Lao Tzu to record his teachings before he left. He then composed in 5,000 characters the Tao Te Ching [The Way and Its Power]).

Self-leaders have a drive for autonomy, can make decisions, are more creative and persist in the face of adversity.

Some of the **intentional behaviours** that characterise self-**leadership** are: self-awareness, **self-goal** setting, self-motivation, positive self-talk, assertive communication and the ability to receive and act on feedback (by moving beyond viewing it only as criticism and not responding with the ego).

Becoming a **self-leader** and maintaining self-leadership is a development activity that you conduct with yourself; but organizations that support and encourage self-leadership reap the benefit.

So, how can we go about mastering ourselves?

Our journey takes us deeper as we get to know ourselves a bit better. Our next steps take us into our childhood where we look at our first basic instincts. When we are born and we first see the light of day, so to speak, we experience a strong instinct for survival and thereafter the need to be cared for. Human babies are very vulnerable and it takes years before we are able to look after ourselves. So what happens with these instincts for survival and the need to be cared for? If these needs are appropriately met during our developmental years then we form a deep sense of security; if not, the converse happens. At the same time we develop our self-esteem. Self-esteem refers to how you feel about yourself overall, how much esteem, positive regard or self-love you have. Self-esteem develops from experiences and situations that have shaped how you view yourself today. Our childhood plays a very important role in this development. (See Appendix A for a brief self- esteem assessment.)

For example, if we received messages in our childhood from our caregivers along the lines of: "You are not good enough; look at your sister/brother/neighbour's child – I wish you could be more like them", then you will have a feeling of inferiority and continually try to prove that you are worthy. You may also resent them and make them the target of your unhappiness. As a young child you do not realise that the problem here lies with the caregiver and that the message they are giving you is a result of their own experiences and feelings, and that it is not necessarily about you at all.

Let us consider another example: if you are spoilt and led to believe that everything you think, say and do is right, without consequences to negative behaviour, then you will grow up believing that the world owes you and that in turn can lead you to become selfish and self-centred.

Now, pause for a moment and consider how the above two mentioned examples will show up in a person's behaviour in the workplace. The "you" in the first example will most probably need to be reassured as he/she could lack self - confidence, whereas in the second example "you" may well have no realistic idea of his/her actual performance and will most probably not be open to honest feedback, because they are always right and know best....

It is therefore very important to reflect on the following:

- What is my self-esteem currently?

_____

_____

_____

- Can I see or understand where my **behaviour** stems from?

  _____

  _____

- Am I able and willing to adjust my behaviour where it does not serve me any longer?

  _____

  _____

- What do I need to let go of, acknowledge or accept in order to adjust my behaviour?

  _____

  _____

Our next step in our journey takes us to the topic of self-**confidence. Self-confidence** is how you feel about your abilities and can vary from situation to situation. I may have healthy self-esteem, but low confidence about **situations** involving mathematics (perhaps due to a lack of skills). Self-confidence often relates to ability and skills or knowledge. If you have a low level of self-confidence it can be addressed by training and coaching in terms of skills improvement. If the ability is low then rather focus on areas where there is an actual aptitude.

When you love **yourself,** your **self-esteem** improves, which helps you in the process of becoming more confident. When you are confident in areas of your life, you begin to increase your overall sense of esteem. You can work on both at the same time.

Our levels of self-esteem and self-confidence show up in the way we lead. The more secure we are in ourselves, the more comfortable we are working with others and allowing others the space to be themselves as well. I have observed over years of working with leaders, that those who have been willing to deal with their personal challenges (such as an abusive childhood or hurtful relationship issues), that they emerge as more compassionate human beings. The manner in which they conduct themselves with others is from a comfortable inner place, which in turn then **positively** affects their **workplace** relationships.

Relationship Building Matrix

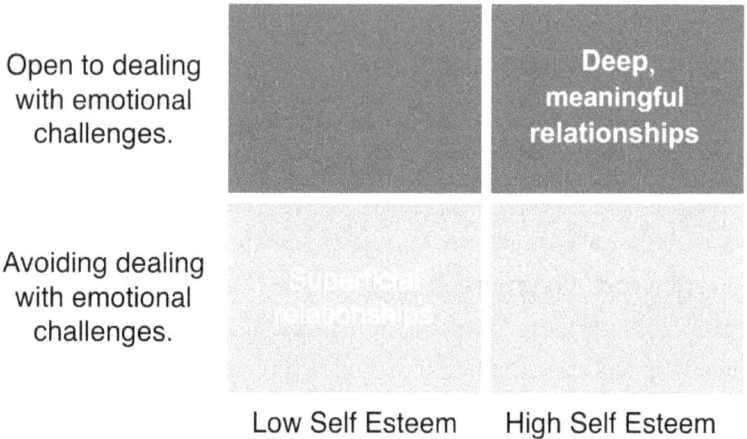

	Low Self Esteem	High Self Esteem
Open to dealing with emotional challenges.		Deep, meaningful relationships
Avoiding dealing with emotional challenges.	Superficial relationships	

In the above diagram the ideal relationship is when a person is open to dealing with emotional challenges and has higher levels of self-esteem resulting in deeper, more meaningful relationships.

Resilience Next I would like to share a story about resilience with you. This story took place during the second world war, when a 24 year old polish Officer, Slavomir Rawicz, was taken to a prisoner of war camp in Siberia. Upon arriving there, this young man determined that he would escape and find his way back home. He started preparing for his escape by saving food and extra clothing and whatever else he thought he might need on his journey. One of his fellow prisoners watched him and decided to join him. He tells his story in a book of his escape and his long journey over many months and across 4000 miles from Yakutsk in Siberia to Northern India. When I read this book I realized once again that resilience can't be taught in books and **classrooms**; life teaches us and **resilience** is the quality we either develop or not when dealing with tough challenges.

"Emotional resilience is the process and outcome of successfully adapting to difficult or challenging life experiences, especially highly stressful or traumatic events." - O'Leary, 1998

In my experience the masterful leaders nearly all have several painful stories to tell of how they dealt with adversity in their lives. They all share an innate sense of optimism, a belief in their own capabilities; they are emotionally hardy and mature, with a positive sense of self and an internal locus of control and responsibility.

I invite you to reflect on the following questions:

- What tough challenges have I had to face in life?

  _____

  _____

- What was my internal dialogue at the time?

  _____

  _____

- How have I made sense of these experiences?

  _____

  _____

- What learning gifts did they provide me with?

  _____

  _____

- Am I able to celebrate these gifts today?

  _____

  _____

- Or do they still trap me **emotionally** and even de-energise me?

  _____

  _____

Creativity is another important topic to discuss. This resides at the heart of a person's childlike sense of wonder and happiness, and is something that you can and should cultivate throughout life. The easiest situation in which to see creativity at work is in children who are happy at play, be it on a sandy beach building sandcastles or playing in mud puddles after spring rains - there is a joyous energy about. We often lose this sense of wonderment as we enter the "hallowed" corridors of corporate life, and more is the pity. The growth of businesses has often relied on a maverick that has made what seemed like a crazy suggestion at the time, **someone** who opened a new opportunity that changed the course of history. Think of the maverick originators of iPod, Facebook, Google and Skype, (Steven Jobs, Mark Zuckerberg, Larry Page & Sergey Brin,

Nicklas Zennstrom and Janus Friis) to name but a few modern-day examples.

So, how do we tap into our creative side if it has been lying dormant for some time?

Choose any creative activity that resonates with you and make sure that you play at it at least once a week, be it woodwork, taking up a musical instrument, attending singing lessons, dancing, art, wood-carving, writing, cooking, gardening....the list is endless. Allow it to be a creative outlet and fun, but beware not to turn it into a competition or a duty as that will defeat the purpose of the exercise, which is to get you in touch with all aspects of yourself. It is thus extremely important that if you are not very successful at it initially, you don't see it as failure but as something you do to please your own desire of being creative, whatever the outcome.

Determination and will power are closely related qualities. How do we achieve anything in life? We must want to do it, and the wanting to do it is linked to our perceived benefits of achieving the goal. For example, if we want to complete our studies, we pursue the end goal in the wish for knowledge of the subject matter and for being able to get a job or create a job. When we exercise, we do it because we feel good afterwards; there are health benefits attached to it and we may be practising for some event. So the perceived benefit to be from the activity must be such that it compels us to complete it. Often when clients share their unaccomplished task with me, the underlying issue is that the reasons for doing it were not compelling enough and the will and determination were not there.

The following provides an opportunity to be curious about your values, because if they are strong enough they will compel you to achieve your goals.

Wearing your self-leadership hat, ask yourself:

- What characteristics about myself do I value the most?

  _____

  _____

  _____

- Why do I value them – what benefit have I derived from them in the past?

  _____

  _____

  _____

- Are there any of my values that no longer serve my **purpose?**

  _____

  _____

  _____

- If so, what are they?

_____

_____

_____

- Do I need to replace any of them? If so which ones? And with what?

_____

_____

_____

As I mentioned at the start of the journey, you are viewed as a holistic person and therefore, to be able to lead yourself you need to address all aspects of yourself. For our next steps we will be considering your mind, body and soul.

Firstly, consider a useful observation made by the Dalai Lama. When asked: "What thing about humanity surprises you the most?" the Dalai Lama answered: "Man....because he sacrifices his health in order to make money. Then he sacrifices money to recuperate his health. And then he is so anxious about the future that he does not enjoy the present; the result being that he does not live in the present or the future; he lives as if he is never going to die, and then dies having never really lived."

So we will **consider** first of all our physical wellbeing. In today's world we live extremely fast-paced lives, whether you live in New York, London, Paris, Hong Kong, Rio de Janeiro or Johannesburg, it is all the same....go, go, go..... Inevitably people suffer from burnout and it affects everyone differently: some experience a breakdown in relationships, some have health problems, some become depressed and some experience all three.

Thus our starting point will be to look at stress, and how to cope with it. We look not at the stress that gently nudges you into action (good stress), but the following three kinds of chronic stress:

- **Physical stress,** which results from **working** beyond one's physical capacity, leaving one tired and exhausted. Counter this by
    - o taking time out to re-charge one's batteries
    - o eating nutritious meals
    - o taking part in physical activities
    - o ensuring restorative sleep

- **Mental stress,** which stems from heavy workloads with tight deadlines – competing with yourself or others leads to mental stress. Counter this by
    - o developing mental mind clearing exercises such as a "to do list" for both work and private actions, write the actions down at the end of the day and keep track of progress
    - o planning to take "mental" breaks; for example an hour before bedtime start slowing down, leave all action lists to the side and do

something relaxing (that does not include your electronics!).

- o leaving your office during lunch time for a change of scenery.

- **Emotional stress,** which is deeply rooted and caused by bad relationships at home or at work. Emotional stress needs to be dealt with by
  - o developing skills to express emotions freely and without fear,
  - o increasing one's ability to release pent-up feelings and emotion.

So, the next question is, if you were to rate your current level of stress on a scale of 1-3, what would it be?

1	=	Low
2	=	**Medium**
3	=	High

Looking at the three areas of stress, namely physical, mental and emotional, can you define what your stressors (those things that cause you to experience stress) currently are?

It is important to be aware of the chemical effects of stress in order to realise the long term effects of prolonged stress.

Stress is **a stimulus** which triggers the **autonomic** nervous system which in turn is activated and releases

- **adrenaline,** which **increases** heart rate and blood pressure and mobilizes energy resources, and
- cortisol, which helps to us to **remember** things and readies the immune system for an attack (this explains why people often get sick after a very stressful event)

Further signs of **overload** show up in one or more of the following ways:

- anxiety attacks
- irritability
- allergic reactions
- **insomnia**
- drinking too much, smoking, overeating, drug abuse
- sadness, depression
- feeling constantly under pressure

It follows that if we have an understanding of the impact that stress has on us physically, mentally and emotionally and we know where our current stressors lie, then we can take positive actions to deal with it, which is part and parcel of self-leadership.

To truly be a leader of oneself it is important to address all areas of one's life, in what I call the Self-leadership Wheel (also discussed in the chapter on Success). For now I want to introduce the various aspects of the wheel to you and ask you to reflect on some questions as we travel through the wheel.

The Self-leadership Wheel is based on a number of wellness aspects as seen in the diagram on the next page. Let's start with understanding the word "Wellness". The word originates from the root word for wholeness which flows from abundance, which is exactly what we need in our lives to become and remain well and whole. Wellness can be defined as the condition of optimum health. It is the integrative blend of physical, intellectual, emotional, social, occupational, financial, environmental and spiritual well-being, a continuous conscious choice which requires personal responsibility and commitment.

Self-Leadership Wheel

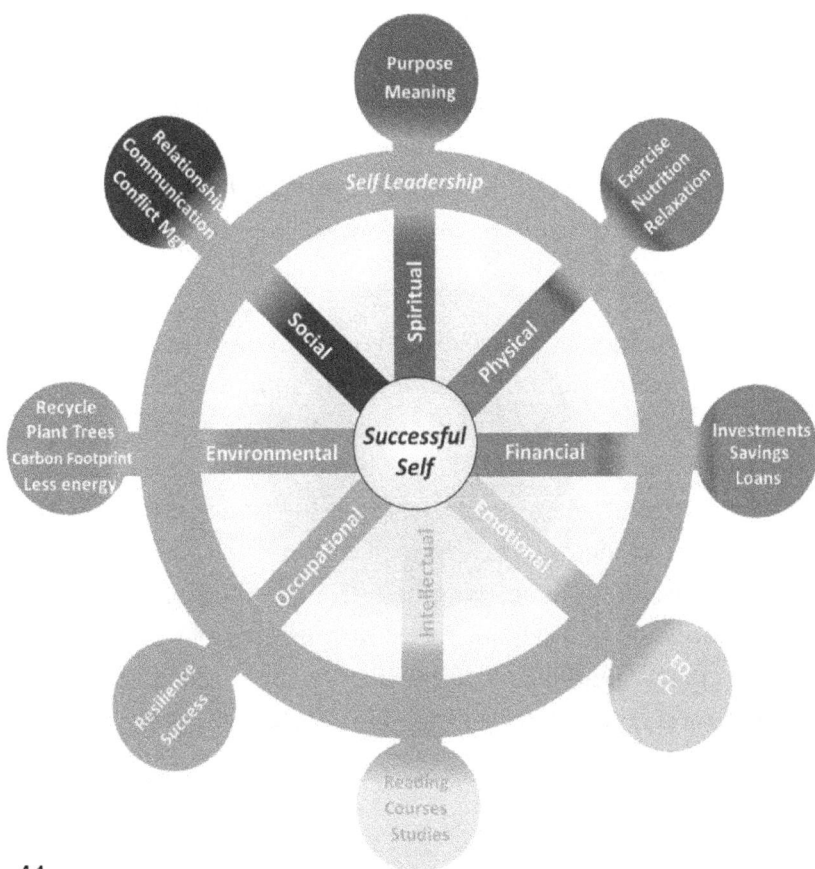

Mental or intellectual wellbeing Our next task is to understand how the mind works, to enable us to manage our thoughts positively. Our mind is constantly busy, like a teenage taxi driver on Prozac, flitting from topic to topic in a never ending stream. What typically happens is that our thoughts are controlling us and not the other way around. So we are either chasing deadlines, planning meetings or, better still, the outcomes of the meetings that haven't even happened yet, and our forthcoming holidays and….and…and… If you were an outsider to your mind, what would you see? Neatly compartmentalised sections or a mad scramble? A tightly controlled, "I will only allow X, Y and Z" or a maze of activity or something in between? How many of us have taken stock and realised that we actually have the ability to become aware of our thoughts and to choose whether they drive us or whether we are going to choose how we handle our thoughts. How do we do that?

Sit still for a moment. Stop all activity. Close your eyes; become aware of your breathing. Keeping your mind focussed on your breathing, become aware of the rise and fall in your chest as you breathe in and out. Take your awareness to your feet. Gently lift your feet up and then place them back onto the floor. Wiggle your toes and place them in a relaxed fashion on the floor. Now, take your awareness to your thoughts. What do you find? Can you see how they flit from subject to subject? To what effect? Gently slow down your breathing, keep slowing it down and allow yourself to relax. What happens to your thoughts as you start to relax?

The purpose of the exercise is for you to become aware of your thoughts, and it is easier if you are more relaxed, especially if this is your first time of consciously doing so. Now, imagine if you can direct your thoughts consciously, daily choosing positive over negative and catching yourself if you have drifted into a quagmire of thoughts.

The ego It would be remiss of me not to mention the ego at this **point**. The ego forms such a constant part of the way in which we operate that more often than not all our actions are coming from our ego. Your ego is your conscious mind, the part of your identity that you consider your "self ". If you say someone has a big *ego*, then you are saying he is too full of himself. If the ego is positively managed then the person is regarded as having good self-esteem; if negatively managed then it shows up as an inflated sense of self, and the person is likely to be judgemental and over critical.

Allow me to share a beautiful story about the ego:

A doll made of salt journeyed for **thousands** of miles and stopped on the edge of the sea.

It was **fascinated** by this moving liquid mass, so unlike anything it had seen before. "What are you?" said the salt doll to the sea. "Come in and see," said the sea with a smile. So the doll waded in. The further it went the more it dissolved until there was only a pinch of it left. Just before it **dissolved** completely, the doll exclaimed in wonder: "Now I know what I am!"

As leaders of self, we need to be **conscious** of our ego and manage it. When it is not managed it can show itself in many ways. For example, our fears and doubts and judgements are all based on the ego. I recall an instance when I had to provide a talk and was well prepared and quite nervous as I had high expectations and wanted to live up to them. The moment I realised that my high expectations were my ego saying, "Are you good enough? Can you do this?", I realised that if I let go and simply did my best and shared what I wanted to share with the audience in a relaxed and open manner, then all would be well. And it was, the moment I let go of my expectations. The ego that is unmanaged creates distance between our deeper, wiser, inner self and other people.

Physical well-being Next we need to look after our physical bodies, nourish them, exercise and relax them to ensure that they are maintained as the vehicles which they are, ready to carry us forth. Suffice it to say that a well-balanced natural diet can affect one's wellbeing positively. A few things to keep in mind are:

- Eat a healthy, balanced diet consisting of three meals a day (do not overeat per meal!).
- Ensure a good supply of protein (not only meat) as it is a blood sugar stabilizer.
- Use scientifically formulated supplementation such as a multivitamin and mineral to ensure that the body is provided with its essentials.
- Drink plenty of water (approximately 1.5 litres per day).

- Eat a variety of foods prepared in a healthy natural manner - the more fresh the better.
- Limit your intake of processed foods and sugar.
- Create a relaxed environment where you eat; make meals a celebration of life.

Some benefits of maintaining a healthy diet are:

- improved concentration and focus
- improved mood stability
- longevity
- more restorative sleep
- improved sustainable energy levels

(See Appendix B for some delicious recipes)

Exercise is another important element in self leadership, as it is linked with the supply of serotonin, the feel-good hormone which is released in the blood stream when exercising. It is useful to combine physical exercises, be it running, swimming, cycling or dancing, with a relaxing practice like yoga or tai chi. Where exercise activates the sympathetic nervous system (our fight and flight response) yoga and tai chi activate the parasympathetic nervous system which deals with our rest and relaxation system. As mentioned previously, in our very hectic lives we need a lot more rest and relaxation.

Sleep is the next topic for consideration. Sleep is essential for our well-being. Too little sleep leaves us feeling irritable and our **immune** system's response is lowered, making us susceptible to disease. Too many of us don't sleep well at night and wake up feeling tired and drained and not ready to go to work in the morning. How can we improve our sleep?

The following are a few tips if you would like to improve the quality of your sleep. I recommend these for the typical work week, Monday to Friday, to ensure maximum output and feeling on top of things.

- Try to go to bed at **a** more or less regular bed time during the week.

- Start slowing down mentally before bedtime:

  o Complete your work and personal "to do" list before you decide it is the end of the day, so that it does not feature in your mind at 2 o' clock in the morning when you should be enjoying good quality sleep.

  o Shut off all electronics, yes ALL!, an hour before sleep.

  o Bath or shower an hour before bedtime to start allowing the body to trigger **relaxation.** You could, for example, have **a** bath with aromatherapy oils and candlelight, with soft music in the background and let yourself soak up the relaxed atmosphere.

  o Read something relaxing before going to sleep.

- Never have complex conversations before **bedtime;** schedule them for a more suitable time.

- Avoid all **stimulants** such as alcohol, coffee, sugar, cigarettes and heavy meals before bedtime, as they will affect the quality of your sleep.

- Keep your bedroom a relaxed place for sleeping and relaxation.

Reflection exercise:

Imagine yourself in detail when you are 100% healthy. How do you feel? Now describe how you look and feel when you are 100% healthy.

_____

_____

_____

Emotional wellbeing is critical for self-leadership, and it is really when we are open and honest with ourselves about how we feel, what affects us, what upsets us, what makes us happy and where we are in our lives emotionally, that we are free from emotional constraints. Emotional wellbeing is literally the foundation upon which everything else rests. The other aspects are all interlinked but without emotional wellbeing the rest matters nought. Like everyone else, I have had my fair share of emotional challenges. They have not been easy to deal with, but over the years I have learned that the only way to deal with anything close to the heart is to face it and work with it until one achieves peace. A mentor of mine always said: "Focus on what you control. Let go of what you don't." Lady Macbeth put it thus: "What is without all remedy should be without regard."

A positive way of dealing with the things we have no control over is to forgive ourselves where relevant and to look for the gift in every situation that aids in our growth. I have learned with the relationships in my life that have presented me with hurt and tears, that they have been my biggest teachers. If I was willing to delve really deeply, I could find the gift of growth inside every single one of them.

Let's explore this with a few thoughts and questions:

- Emotionally speaking, what are the biggest and most valuable lessons that you have learned over the years?

  _____

  _____

  _____

- Who taught them to you?

_____

_____

_____

- Can you forgive those who have hurt you over the years?

_____

_____

_____

- Can you forgive yourself?

_____

_____

_____

- Can you appreciate the gifts that you **received** from everyone and see that the gifts have made you a richer person?

_____

_____

_____

The mind (our thoughts), the body (our physical wellbeing) and our **emotions** work together and affect us in an interconnected way. For example, if I have experienced an intense emotionally upheaval, a week later I will experience cold/flu-like symptoms as my immune system responds with approximately a week's delay. When I was younger I seldom expressed my feelings and this resulted in me often getting a sore throat that would in severe circumstances become **tonsillitis**. I have learned to be aware of my emotions and to express them so as not to cause physical illness. This is an ongoing process and requires patience. There are two books in the recommended reading section if you are interested in this **topic**. (Louise Hay and Debbie Shapiro's work.)

Occupational wellbeing speaks to how you choose to make a living. Most of us spend most of our lives at work. Would it not make sense to make the experience as enjoyable as possible? All jobs have aspects that we can really enjoy and aspects that don't necessarily appeal to us, but we know we have to do them. So whether you work for as an employee in a corporate entity, or as a volunteer in a non-profit organisation, or you are an entrepreneur, it is all the same. Our attitude plays a very important part in how we show up at work and how our colleagues and bosses see us, respond to us and treat us. Thus, it is not just a matter of jumping ship the moment you don't "like" where you are, as you might find the same challenges at the environment where you move to. My recommendation is to make the most of where you are, tackle the challenges and, in Mahatma Ghandi's words, be the change that you wish to see in the world.

Some questions for reflection are:

- What can you do differently or better at work than you are currently doing, so that you may add value to your
  - o job,
  - o colleagues,
  - o bosses,
  - o **employees?**

  _____

  _____

  _____

- What shift is **required** inside you to change your attitude to a positive one (if it is not positive already)?

  _____

  _____

  _____

- Are you able to make this shift?

  _____

  _____

  _____

Social wellbeing is important for all of us as no man or woman is an island. Social interaction is one of our basic needs. In South Africa we have the idea of "Ubuntu", which in essence means "I am because you are". We are born into communities: our family and friends and the broader communities where we live. In many instances we have lost our sense of community and we have become isolated. In the past, there was a saying that applied: "It takes a village to raise a child", meaning that everyone in the community played a part in the raising of a child and many 'villagers' were necessary to raise a child properly. Nowadays it is mostly done in a nuclear family setup. Imagine the different pressures in just this one activity. When the entire community played a part, the child had the benefit of the communal wisdom and gained different perspectives. In a nuclear family, the perspectives are very limited. So what do we do? We create our own communities around work, hobbies, **spiritual** gatherings, **interests** and **especially electronics.** We interact with people, some of us **requiring** more **interaction** than others. There is no right or wrong way and it is more a matter of what works for you and a question of whether you feel sufficiently connected to others so as not to feel isolated. (More will be provided on this in the chapters on relationships.)

Some reflection questions are:

- Are you engaging with those around you in a meaningful way?

_____

_____

_____

- If not, what can you do to change this?

_____

_____

_____

- If you feel lonely and isolated, can you join an activity or society in order to explore this aspect of yourself?

_____

_____

_____

Financial wellbeing deals with your ability to look after yourself financially. I have personally experienced the gravity of the words financial independence as I have worked in the corporate world and been full-time employed (Oh! the joys of receiving a guaranteed salary!). I have also been in a business partnership that resulted in total financial ruin and I have had to work my way back to financial well-being as an entrepreneur in tough market conditions. So, I cannot talk about self-leadership without addressing financial well-being. Financial well-being is more than just whether you can meet or exceed your monthly budget, whether you have enough saved for your retirement, or whether you have investments that are growing over time; it also has to do with how you value money and what your personal 'connection' to money is. Do you see it as a vehicle of enablement or do you see it as a necessary evil? The way in which you view money will have a direct impact on how you value it and how you interact with it. I see it as a valuable currency and a positive agent of empowerment and I believe in abundance, in the sense that there is more than enough for everyone.

Reflection questions:

- How do you view money?
    - An enabler?
    - A necessary evil?

_____

_____

_____

- Do you believe
    - there is more than enough to go around?
    - you have to cling to every last cent?

_____

_____

_____

- Do you treat your money with
    - respect?
    - disrespect?

_____

_____

_____

- What do you want to change in the way in which you regard money?

_____

_____

_____

Environmental wellbeing speaks to how we take care of our environment to ensure that we leave it in a healthy state for the generations to come. The world has grown and expanded at an alarming rate over the last few decades. We are sitting with a world population exceeding seven billion people. We, the seven billion, are taking away from the environment at an alarming rate, like swarming locusts. So we need to stop and take note to act urgently in a responsible manner to limit our impact on the environment. I often go to the South African bush for a retreat, I call it my soul retreat, where we have solar power and gas and very little else (thus no electronics). It is here where we have to pack all our food and clear away our rubbish that I realise what we generate and I am always humbled when I leave as I watch how the antelope, rhino, lions, elephants and even the small insects operate in their habitat. They are such brilliant teachers, and I try to learn from them and remember their example of nature conservation when I return to urban life.

Some reflection questions:

- Are you aware of the impact your daily life has on the environment?

  _____

  _____

- What can you do daily to make a positive difference?

  _____

  _____

- Will you be willing to do it?

  _____

  _____

- What do you think your future self will tell the children that are yet to be born, about the environment?

  _____

  _____

Spiritual wellbeing: Finally, our solemn thought to conclude this chapter is around our spiritual compass that guides us and reminds us that there is so much more to life than the material world in which we live.

Here are some **questions** to guide your **thinking** and for **reflection**:

- What anchors you in life?

  _____

  _____

  _____

- What gives meaning to your life?

_____

_____

_____

- What is your spiritual life like – is it rich and do you pay it attention daily?

_____

_____

_____

- Is it uplifting and does it act as a guiding light or inner compass?

_____

_____

_____

- How does this influence your day-to-day life and your values?

_____

_____

_____

- Can you allow others their spiritual views even if they differ from yours?

_____

_____

_____

Summary Box:

The self-leadership journey has shown you the key qualities required for your self-leadership toolkit, namely self-esteem, self-confidence, resilience, determination and will power, creativity and the self-leadership wheel and its various aspects. Our understanding of how we respond to and manage stress is also useful as we go through changes continuously and we inevitably experience stress. Knowing how to deal constructively with stress is essential if we are to be capable of dealing with change, growth and everyday life.

Chapter 5. Success

"Whatever you can do, or dream you can, begin it. Boldness has genius, power and magic in it."

In this chapter we will explore what success means to you. How do we define success and explore its various facets? We need to choose the main goals we would like to work on and commit to them. As this is an ongoing process, we all need to revisit this as the months go past, and as you continue to achieve your goals and new goals become relevant. You may even find that your definition of success changes over time.

What is success? How do we measure success? What works for one person does not necessarily work for another. It is important that we reflect on what success means to you, because the way in which you measure your success in terms of self-leadership will determine how you feel about yourself and consequently how you behave and respond towards others.

There is a lovely story about success that I would like to share with you. It is the story about a farmer's widow, Anna Mary Moses. By the time she was 78 years old she suffered so badly from arthritis that she had to stop crocheting and decided to take up painting instead. She painstakingly taught herself to paint, and she painted and she painted until she decided that she was ready and that she would exhibit her work at the local arts and crafts market. As luck and providence would have it, a New York art dealer was travelling the country in search of new talent. He saw her work, fell in love with it and offered her a one woman show in his New York art gallery. The rest, as they say, is history. Before her death at the age of 101, she had painted over a 1000 paintings. She even featured on the cover of Life Magazine. I love this story, firstly because generally none of my corporate clients are 78 years old and this is a story not of an athletic superstar, pop star or movie star, but of an ordinary person, who humbly did something extraordinary. So what is there to fear for any of us? We must simply be who we are, as Anna Mary Moses was.

WWW.PAINTINGSELECT.COM
FINE ART REPRODUCTIONS

Reflection exercise:

Pause and reflect on what success means to you. Identify all aspects of what would constitute success for you. Write them down.

We are now ready to travel the journey even deeper and I invite you to complete the exercise of plotting yourself on the Self-leadership Wheel. Reflect on where you currently find yourself. Simply be honest with yourself.

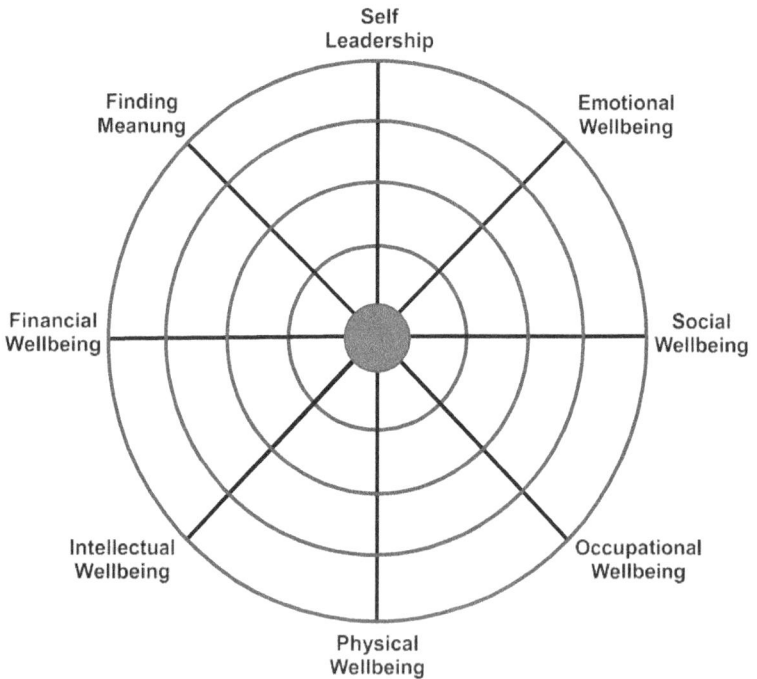

Reflection exercise: Self-leadership Wheel

To reflect on the spokes of your wheel, draw four circles on your paper and give each area/spoke a score ranging from 0 to 5 (you can even use half values), depending on how satisfied you are with each of these areas of your life:

0 = Not satisfied (the inner ring)

3 = Medium level of satisfaction

5 = Very satisfied (the outer ring)

Once you have completed the Self-leadership wheel, you can connect all the dots to provide an overall picture. Then choose the key areas (preferably not more than 3) which you would like to work on. Choose the areas according to the impact you feel they will have on your life if you were to address them **now**. Once you have addressed them, you choose the next areas and so on. The process below illustrates one area that was chosen, namely learn to manage stress, under the area of physical wellbeing, and then the questions in the five columns were applied accordingly. Do the same with your three areas, making sure that you answer all the questions in each area. The two questions in the last column consolidate your reasons for wanting to take action and bring about a positive change in your life.

Self-Leadership Wheel

Write down your personal goals	How long have you had this goal?	What is the biggest stumbling block that prevents you from achieving it?	What have you done in the last 24 hours to achieve it?	What about this goal compels you to achieve it? How will you feel once you have achieved it?
E.g. Learn to manage stress	10 Years	Inability to implement – not knowing what to do	Learning how to implement stress management techniques	Improvement in my overall health – I will feel more energetic and in control

_____

_____

_____

_____

_____

As you have noticed, the self-leadership journey is ongoing, in which we continue to strive to know ourselves from one year to the next, allowing us to grow and develop. So keep track of your goals and develop them as you go along.

Finally, I want to **conclude** this chapter of our journey by sharing with you the most beautiful definition of success that resonates deeply with me.

"To laugh often and much, to win the respect of intelligent people and the affection of children; to earn the appreciation of honest critics and endure the betrayal of false friends; to appreciate beauty, to find the best in others; to leave the world a bit better, whether by a healthy child, a garden, or a redeemed social condition; to know even one life has breathed easier because you have lived. This is to have succeeded"
-Ralph Waldo Emerson

(Ralph Waldo Emerson (May 25, 1803 – April 27, 1882) was an American essayist, lecturer and poet, who led the Transcendentalist movement of the mid-19th century.)

Summary box:

You have defined success and chosen your main goals to work on. Now work with the process over time and enjoy the results.

Chapter 6. Obstacles and imperfections

*"**Character** cannot be developed in ease and quiet. Only through experience of trial and suffering can the soul be strengthened, ambition inspired, and success achieved."* - Helen Keller

In this chapter you will have an opportunity to see how you address obstacles and how to improve on the way you deal with them. We also explore our view on so-called imperfections and realise how we regard them in our lives. We consider the choices with regard to our imperfections and how we deal with them to ensure we move forward and embrace all that is.

What prevents us from being the best that we can be? Where do our fears come from? What holds us back?

Over the years working with my clients and myself (a constant work in progress, I admit) I have noticed that we all have the same fears.

FEAR the disabler:

F alse

E vidence

A ppearing

R eal

We become handicapped by our fears. Typically, they are the fear of

- failure
- commitment
- not being good enough
- loss
- success

How can we overcome these fears?

Firstly, we need to realise that our fears are directly linked to our egos. (Please note that I am not referring here to any life threatening fears). Allow me to explain. Let us look, for example, at our fear of failure. It links us directly to our ego and judgement as we are subjected to the internal questions of "Can I succeed?" and "What if I don't?" These questions are all about judgement. Surely we are so much more than this? What would happen if we rather reframed our fear of failure into: "What can I learn about myself today?" or "What if just being the real me is good enough? The moment we relax the ego, we take the pressure off ourselves and are present in the moment. The real you shows up. How does that feel instead? More empowering and much less judgemental, I believe. Are you able to offer that space to someone else too?

As we grow in our being and we face our fears as they arise, when they arise, we become freer in ourselves and allow others to express and be themselves too. What an incredible gift that is, not only to you but also to those around you.

I want to end this section with the words of **Marianne** Williamson about success: *"Our deepest fear is not that we are inadequate. Our deepest fear is that we are powerful beyond measure. It is our light, not our darkness that most frightens us. We ask ourselves, 'Who am I to be brilliant, gorgeous, talented, and fabulous?' Actually, who are you not to be? You are a child of God. Your playing small does not serve the world. There is nothing enlightened about shrinking so that other people won't feel insecure around you. We are all meant to shine, as children do. We were born to manifest the glory of God that is within us. It's not just in some of us; it's in everyone. And as we let our own light shine, we unconsciously give other people permission to do the same. As we are liberated from our own fear, our presence automatically liberates others."*

Imperfections

We can begin the discussion on imperfections by considering the following story:

A man who took great pride in his lawn one day suddenly found himself with a large crop of dandelions. He tried every method he knew to destroy them. Still they plagued him.

Finally he wrote to the Department of Agriculture. He enumerated all the things he had tried and closed his letter with the question: 'What shall I do now?' In due course the reply came: 'We suggest you learn to love them.'

I was proud of my lawn but I too was plagued with dandelions that I kept fighting with every means in my power. So learning to love them was no easy task. I began by talking to them each day. Cordial. Friendly. They maintained a sullen silence. They were smarting from the war I had waged against them- and were suspicious of my motives.

But the day came when they smiled. And relaxed. And we started to be friends.

My lawn, of course, was ruined. But how attractive my garden became!

In our current world where we are so obsessed with perfection, or our idea of perfection, that we go to great lengths and expense to achieve it. We have lost the road as we chase after empty ideals; the number of people on anti-depressants has never been so high and it is growing still. So, one should pause and ask oneself…Why is this the case? People are feeling disconnected and on the treadmill of life, chasing faster and faster. What are they chasing and for whose benefit? Through my leadership development work I have realised that people start chasing an external vision of an ideal, based on the media or what peers or family members say, or to cover up their own insecurities. In the end this causes a level of disconnection with themselves and they then try to fill this void with "things".

"Things" can take the shape of material goods, easy relationships, chasing promotions and power, and so forth….the nett result remains the same, they end up feeling 'hollow" inside and not liking themselves or the lives they have created for themselves. Self-leadership is also about facing what we deem as our imperfections. What would happen if we stood still and really got to know our so-called imperfections? What is there to celebrate about them? How can we use them positively in our lives, rather than avoiding them, **ignoring** them or pretending they are not there?

One of my own deep insecurities has been the nagging question as to whether I am good enough. This stemmed from being in awe of my very, very intelligent father. He **achieved** two Doctorates and several degrees in his life, had a photographic memory, was sporty, well read and well-travelled, and was a warm and outgoing person. It was his intellectual capacity that I admired so much and I would push myself to excel, wanting his approval. This continued subconsciously throughout my life until one day I saw it for what it was and decided that my best was good enough for me. I did not need my father's or anyone else's approval. I can achieve for the sake of enjoying the achievement for itself and learning new and wonderful things along the way. I am still driven, but it now has a different flavour and I can laugh at myself when I see this insecurity kick in. This is still a work in progress, but I now have a sense of humour around it.

My next invitation to you is reflect on:

- What are your so-called imperfections?

_____

_____

- Can you identify where they originate from?

_____

_____

_____

- Can you come to terms with them?

_____

_____

_____

- What do you need to do to cause a shift in how you deal with them?

_____

_____

_____

Summary box:

You have learnt that obstacles are based on our fears and how we deal with fear in our lives. You had the opportunity to explore where your fears come from and how to deal with them going forward. Finally, you had a look at your attitude and beliefs around imperfections and your level of compassion towards yourself and others.

Chapter 7. Relationships

"Real magic in relationships means an absence of judgement of others." Wayne Dyer.

In this chapter we look at how we relate to **ourselves,** how comfortable we are in our own skin, and how developing a closer relationship with ourselves can impact on how we relate to others.

The word relationship denotes how one or more people connect with each other.

How do we relate to ourselves? That is the key to all our other relationships. Do we care for ourselves and do we like and love ourselves? Are we kind to ourselves? I can sense some of you cringe when I ask these questions. Don't worry. The truth is that we all battle with this and it is not an egotistical exercise at all, indeed it is a very gentle and deep exercise of looking ourselves squarely in the eye. It is a matter of taking stock. We tend to place our focus external to ourselves because it is just so much easier. Yet, when relationships fail we blame others, or circumstances or our upbringing.

How often do we stop and pause and really give **ourselves** some deep air time to connect with our fears (the previous chapter), with our dreams (the chapter on success) and with what we have to offer in relationships and what our expectations are. So, with the focus of this journey on self-leadership, we look at our relationship with ourselves. If we are okay with ourselves and we like and even love ourselves we bring ourselves forth or forward to different opportunities of relating and having relationships that could be meaningful on so many different levels.

The key questions concerning relationships are: "Do I trust myself?" and "Do I trust others?" The answers reveal how you are likely to relate to others. The more you trust yourself, the more confident you will be in your relationships with others. The more you trust others, the better you will be able to relate to them. A lack of trust, both of yourself and others, is a sign and a cause of insecurity and needs to be addressed.

Some self-reflection questions:

- What aspects of myself do I approve of?

  _____

  _____

  _____

  _____

- What aspects of myself am I not happy with?

  _____

  _____

  _____

  _____

- What can I do about them?

  _____

  _____

  _____

  _____

- In what ways am I distrustful of myself?

  _____

  _____

  _____

  _____

- What can I do about this?

  _____

  _____

  _____

  _____

- What is it about other people that I tend to mistrust?

  _____

  _____

  _____

- What expectations can I let go of to give myself permission to be me?

_____

_____

_____

Summary box:

You looked at how you relate to yourself and whether you like, love and accept yourself. Also, you looked at exploring the opportunities that exist in altering your relationship with yourself, making it more meaningful and seeing how that will impact on how you relate to others.

Chapter 8. Communication

"Tell me and I will forget. Show me and I might remember. Involve me and I will understand." - Benjamin Franklin.

In this chapter we touch on communication: how we communicate with ourselves, getting in touch with our inner voices and learning to deal with them. We also look at two communication models, one that looks at the process and one that deals with the effects of communication.

Communication, our inner communication with ourselves and how we communicate with others, is key to the quality of our relationships. So, if we were to unpack communication, what would it look like? Yes, it is about the message that we share, how we share it and how it is received. For example, if we just refer to the spoken word, then you need to consider with whom you are sharing your message. Do you speak the same language? Do you use jargon specific to your area of expertise? I joined an IT firm and during the first few weeks I discovered an entire new vocabulary.

Our body language and tone of voice are also critical. More than 80% of our communication is related to body language and tone of voice. In other words, our bodies speak more clearly than all the words we could dream of using.

The quality of our listening further **influences** how we communicate. If we are focussed on our own agenda, then the level at which we communicate will be weak as the person with whom you are communicating will get the message, "I am not that important; she has already made up her mind about what she wants." Don't underestimate others' ability to sense this.

People don't care about us until they feel we care about them, so that is the essence of how we should communicate, in both our personal and professional lives.

If we were to look at the various levels of listening alone, it would look like the following, starting at level 1 and moving up to level 5, where we are really listening:

Level 1: Ignoring

Making no effort to listen

Level 2: Pretending

Giving the appearance you are listening, e.g." Uh-huh" (Husbands are often accused of this level of listening.)

Level 3: Selective

Hearing only certain parts that interest you (Wives are often accused of this level of listening.)

Level 4: Attentive

Paying attention, focusing and comparing to your own experience

Level 5: Empathic

Listening to understand the words, intent and feelings

The diagram below is a summary view of communication, showing that it takes place within a context. The sender and the receiver take part in a feedback loop where the message travels via a communication channel. The communication channel can be anything ranging from a face to face interaction to a text message.

Communication

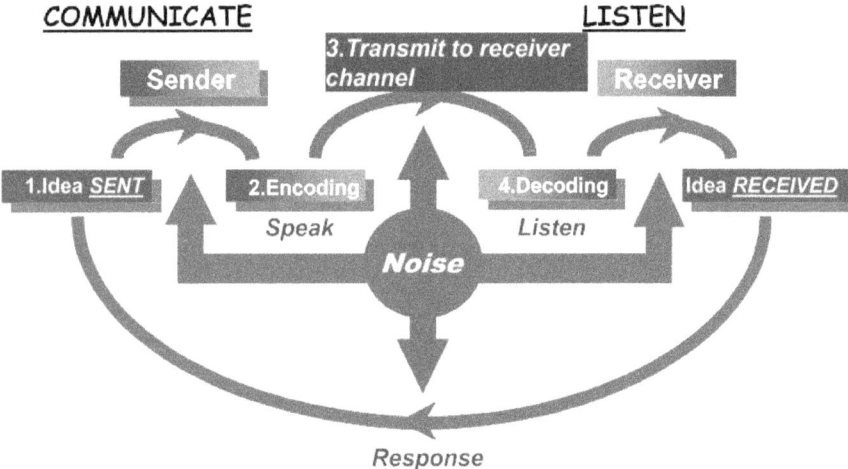

COMMUNICATE

LISTEN

Sender

3.Transmit to receiver channel

Receiver

1.Idea *SENT*

2.Encoding

Speak

4.Decoding

Listen

Idea *RECEIVED*

Noise

Response

You can see from the model above that both sender and receiver have "noise" to filter through before the message can fall on fertile ground. Noise can take on the form of:

- our personal prejudices (culture, likes, dislikes, gender, race, background, religion, values)
- our personal agenda
- our attitude towards the person and the situation/organisation/group
- how we feel (physically, mentally, emotionally)
- unfinished business/issues
- pre-conceived ideas

As you can see, communication is a complex topic, yet it is the key to self-leadership, because we need to be aware of how we communicate, not just with ourselves but to the world at large, as this influences our relationships.

When we become more connected with our inner selves, we are able to connect more profoundly with others. If we apply this to our world of work, where we spend most of our time, would it not make sense to be more effective?

Thinking Win/Win

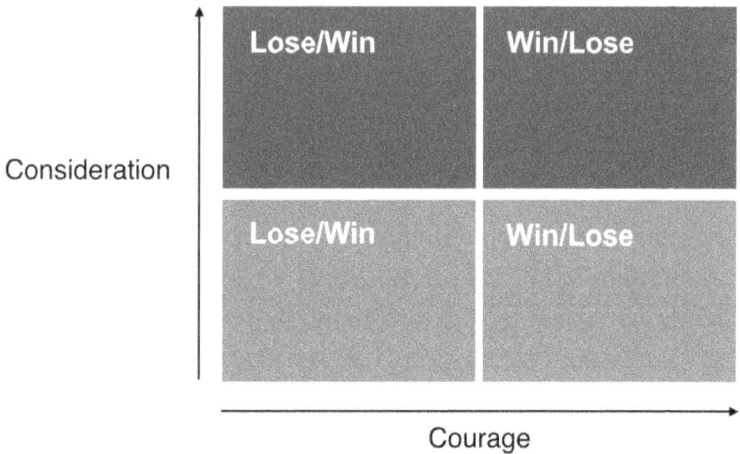

This communication model shows that we have a number of choices when communicating with others. We can choose the least empowered and sustainable way, which is the lose/lose option. Here both parties feel disempowered. The win/lose option is where one person wins and one loses in a case of: "I win, you lose". It may be a situation that requires you to be courageous and ensure that the other person loses. The lose/win scenario requires you to be considerate and allow the other person to win and you to lose. Finally, the optimal choice is where you aim for a win/win scenario. Both parties walk away satisfied. This is ideal if you are looking at a situation where you want a sustainable solution, whether personal or professional.

Some reflection questions in this regard could be:

- How comfortable are you with yourself?

  _____

  _____

  _____

- How honest are you with yourself?

  _____

  _____

  _____

- How effectively do you communicate with others?

  _____

  _____

  _____

- What feedback do you have to confirm this?

  _____

  _____

  _____

- Would you like to improve?

  _____

  _____

  _____

- How would you like to accomplish this improvement?

  _____

  _____

  _____

Our inner voices Yes, you heard correctly, the voices inside your head. If you ask which ones, the voice in your head that answers – that is the one. Here is the good news: you are not going crazy. We all have voices inside our head and we would like sometimes to quieten their chatter. However, until we have mastered that technique, I suggest you befriend them, identify them and let them work for you instead of against you. For example, you may have a voice inside your head that encourages you to do positive and **sometimes** even great things. You probably also have a negative voice that discourages you and puts doubt in your mind. You may have a voice of wisdom that could be the voice of your grandfather or grandmother, and so on.

For now, simply become aware of the voices, quieten the negative voice and grow the positive voice. Just by being aware of the impact that your inner voices can have in your life, you can take charge and guide yourself better.

Self- reflection questions:

- What are the main voices and their characteristics?

  _____

  _____

  _____

- Which of these voices hold you back?

  _____

  _____

  _____

- Which one has the words of wisdom?

  _____

  _____

  _____

- What can you do to still the voices that hold you back and increase the voices of encouragement?

_____

_____

_____

Summary box:

We dealt with communication with others and with ourselves and our inner voices. We looked at a communication model that illustrates the various aspects to be aware of when we communicate. We explored the five levels of listening. We dealt with the effects of our communication. We learned that communication is key to how we express ourselves in relationships.

---

dearest

Chapter 9. Conflict

"All conflict we experience in the world is a conflict within our own selves." - Brenda Shoshanna

For the purposes of self-leadership, we will focus on conflict through the lens of how you handle inner conflict and where it stems from. We will then look at how that impacts on how you handle conflict with others.

Conflict arises when we don't get what we want or we feel **threatened** for some or other reason. Maslow's hierarchy of needs is useful in providing a deeper understanding that will improve your ability to deal with conflict in the future.

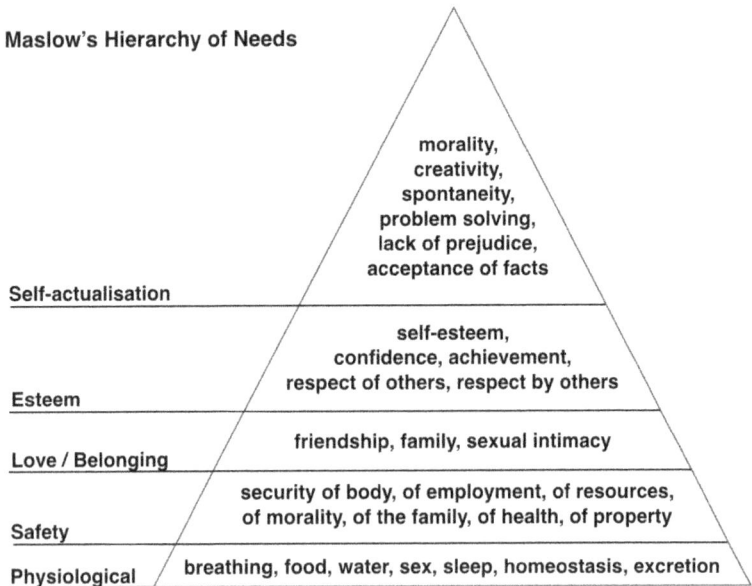

Maslow's Hierarchy of Needs

morality,
creativity,
spontaneity,
problem solving,
lack of prejudice,
acceptance of facts

Self-actualisation

self-esteem,
confidence, achievement,
respect of others, respect by others

Esteem

friendship, family, sexual intimacy

Love / Belonging

security of body, of employment, of resources,
of morality, of the family, of health, of property

Safety

Physiological / breathing, food, water, sex, sleep, homeostasis, excretion

My thinking behind why people have conflict, based on Maslow's hierarchy, is as follows: we all find that our needs are matched somewhere on Maslow's hierarchy; there is no right or wrong, it is simply a matter of where you find yourself currently. You move up or down the hierarchy depending on how your needs are being met at the time. Let me explain what happens when a need is not met, and how this can lead to conflict. Consider a situation where you perceive a threat to a member of your family. For example, a shop assistant did not treat your beloved elderly father well. Immediately you would want to go into the store and address the situation. If you go in aggressively and confront the assistant shouting, without getting the facts, only to discover that their father had very recently passed away, your dad had reminded her of her own father and she was simply trying to get him served as quickly as possible so as to keep it together and not to burst into tears, you will feel terrible, embarrassed and regretful.

I used this particular example, as often in life, if we just had to pause and find out the real facts behind the conflict and dig deeper, we can patiently resolve it. However, too often we get onto our high horse without all the information and then we simply add fuel to the flames.

Isaac Newton's law of "for every action there is an opposite reaction of the same strength" bears out what happens in most conflict situations.

You can take any of the needs on the Maslow hierarchy and apply an example of a need that is not fulfilled, whether real or perceived and see how people respond. When you are confronted with a response from someone and it appears on the surface not to make sense, then dig a bit deeper into understanding the unfulfilled need that may be the trigger causing the inappropriate response.

So what can we do to handle conflict better?

First of all, become calm, really calm, and ground yourself. (You can do this by connecting with your senses. For example, become aware of your breathing - when you are angry your breathing will tend to be rapid. The moment you shift your **awareness** to your breathing, you can slow it down intentionally. Allow a few moments for your breathing to slow down.) Then get all the information about the situation. Dig deeper to see if you can uncover what the underlying issue/s is/are, as they are most often not the obvious one presented as the reason for the conflict. Deal with the real underlying issue by asking all the parties what their interests are and what outcome they are hoping to achieve. Often, if there is a common goal or outcome, it is much easier to resolve the conflict.

The following are a few tips to keep in mind when facing a conflict situation:

- When tired, rather put a watchdog before your mouth; you don't want to say something you are going to regret later.
- Be patient, with yourself and others.
- Distinguish between the person and the behavior.
- Forgive, forget and apologise if you are wrong.

- Keep promises once made.
- Live, Love and Listen.
- Be sincere and honest.

Some reflection questions:

- When looking at Maslow's hierarchy – where do you find yourself currently?

  _____

  _____

  _____

- What are your current trigger points for conflict?

  _____

  _____

  _____

- What can you do to feel more secure and less conflict prone?

  _____

  _____

  _____

- Can you do so now?

_____

_____

_____

Summary box:

We had a look at conflict and explored it through Maslow's hierarchy to see that conflict often arises due to real or perceived needs not met. We explored how we can deal with conflict.

---

dearest

Top Ten Tips of Self-leadership:

- Know who and what you are and be true to yourself.
- Spend quiet time by yourself, regularly.
- Listen and respond to your heart, mind and body.
- Be good to yourself.
- Be brutally honest with yourself; after all, no person knows you better than you know yourself.
- Treat others as you would like them to treat you, with respect, compassion and kindness.
- Give of yourself, your time and attention.
- Spend quality time with your loved ones; they are your greatest support. Show them you value them.
- Be courageous and open to personal growth – you will always feel alive from within.
- There is no failure in life, only feedback. Allow yourself and others to grow.

dearest

Chapter 10. Beyond Self-leadership

*"Life isn't about finding yourself. It is about creating **yourself.**"*
George Bernard Shaw

So, dear fellow **traveller,** we have come to the end of this particular journey. Thank you for walking it with me. I hope that you have gained new insights and that you are able to walk a bit slower, with more comfort and a sense of self-knowing. Sometimes you may know your destination and at other times your destination may be unclear. Use the exercises provided in this book to assist you along your journey, creatively exploring new and better ways of doing things and making modifications along the way as you discover new things about yourself and others.

Before I leave you I want to share with you the knowledge that knowing yourself well can unleash limitless possibilities. I know that the inner journey is not always easy, but the rewards more than make up for the trials and tribulations that we have to go through to get to understand ourselves better.

I would wish that you also celebrate your life. How do you celebrate? At the end of this journey, having completed it successfully, I want you to celebrate it in a way that honours you as a person and makes you feel deeply valued.

I will share with you one way in which I love to celebrate. A special meal, lovingly home cooked, sitting under the stars, with candle light and some flowers on a beautifully laid table, sharing not only my moments but those of my loved ones.

When we raise our glasses, we give grateful thanks to all who have made our journeys possible, in spirit and in life.

I salute you.

dearest

Chapter 11. References and recommended further reading

Emotional Intelligence by Daniel Goleman

Working with Emotional Intelligence by Daniel Goleman

There is a spiritual solution to every problem by Wayne W Dyer

The power of now by Eckhart Tolle

Your body speaks your mind by Debbie Shapiro

Man's search for meaning by Viktor E Frankl

The art of possibility by Rosamund and Benjamin Zander

You can heal your life by Louise Hay

The Long Walk by Slavomir Rawicz

The Seven Habits of Highly Effective People by Stephen R Covey

Chapter 12. Appendix A. Self-esteem questionnaire

SENSE OF SELF / SELF ESTEEM

Answer this questionnaire as honestly as you can.

	Yes	No
I am optimistic.	___	___
I trust my intuition.	___	___
I believe in myself.	___	___
The world is a beautiful place.	___	___
I express my feelings easily.	___	___
It's okay to be angry.	___	___
I can allow myself to feel sad.	___	___
I am good at making decisions.	___	___
I can say "no" when I want to.	___	___
It's okay for me to make mistakes.	___	___
I deserve the best that life has to offer.	___	___

Self- Reflection:

How do you feel when you respond to these questions?

_____

_____

Confident or insecure and uncertain?

_____

_____

If insecure and uncertain, why do you think you feel that way?

_____

_____

Chapter 13. Appendix B. Recipes

Lovingly prepared nutritious meals for the working person

Vegetable Lentil soup (Serves 4)

2 teaspoons vegetable oil	1 onion, diced
2 teaspoons curry powder	1 cup red lentils
1 litre vegetable stock	425g can crushed tomatoes
1 cup water	2 medium potatoes, diced
2 medium carrots, diced	1 cup frozen peas

- Heat oil in a large, deep pan; add onion and sauté until softened. Add the curry powder and stir over heat for a further 2 minutes until fragrant.
- Stir in lentils, stock, **tomatoes,** water, diced potatoes and **carrots.** Bring to boil, and then reduce heat to low and simmer ingredients, covered, for 15-20 minutes.
- Add frozen peas and simmer for a further 5 minutes, or until the vegetables and lentils are tender. Season the soup to taste with salt and pepper and serve with fresh, crusty bread.

Poached fish with lemon grass and ginger

(Serves 4)

4 x 150 g firm white fish fillets (e.g. Hake)

For the poaching liquid	2 cups water
3 lemon grass stalk, bruised	1 garlic clove, chopped

A 5 cm piece fresh ginger, peeled and sliced

3 lime leaves	1 tablespoon fish sauce
2 tablespoons soy sauce	2 teaspoons sugar

To Serve

4 heads bok choy, steamed	400 g egg noodles
Red chilli chopped	Fresh coriander

- Add all the poaching liquid ingredients to a pot. Stir well and bring to a simmer.
- Add the fish fillets and poach for 5-7 minutes or until cooked through. Remove with a slotted spoon and set aside. Strain liquid and keep warm.
- Place noodles and bok choy in a serving bowl, top with fish and ladle over strained cooking liquid. Garnish with fresh chilli and coriander.

Chocolate mousse

(Serves 12)

1x 125g slab milk chocolate

1x125g slab dark chocolate

½ cup brandy (use a 1/3 cup milk with 1 tsp vanilla essence if you don't want to use the brandy)

8 eggs separated

- Melt the chocolate in a double boiler, or very carefully microwave, getting it out and stirring constantly. Stir in the brandy and beaten eggs.
- Halve the mixture, and add an extra 2 tsp cocoa powder to one half.
- Beat the egg whites stiffly, and add ½ to each of the two bowls. Pour into little ramekins or big bowls and refrigerate until set – about 3 hours.